U.S. Fish & Wildlife Service

Private and Public Land Use by Hunters

Addendum to the 2001 National Survey of Fishing, Hunting, and Wildlife-Associated Recreation

Report 2001-8

I0439104

U.S. Fish & Wildlife Service

Private and Public Land Use by Hunters

Addendum to the 2001 National Survey of Fishing, Hunting, and Wildlife-Associated Recreation

Report 2001-8

June 2005

Richard Aiken
Division of Federal Assistance
U.S. Fish and Wildlife Service
Arlington, Virginia

This report complements the National and State Reports for the 2001 National Survey of Fishing, Hunting, and Wildlife-Associated Recreation. The conclusions in this report are the author's and do not represent official positions of the U.S. Fish and Wildlife Service.

The author thanks Sylvia Cabrera and Jerry Leonard for valuable comments on early drafts.

Contents

Introduction

The choice of hunting area is a vital consideration for all hunters. Knowing where the game are is only half the decision; access to the area where the game can be found is also important. There are two possibilities of areas to hunt: publicly owned land and privately owned land. In this report, publicly owned land refers to land owned by federal, state, or local governments. Publicly owned land usually is available to all, but its extent varies by state. Privately owned land refers to all other land, with a focus on land available for hunting. Privately owned land is available to its owner and anyone else who has the owner's permission.

This analysis examines the participation levels, socioeconomic characteristics, and expenditure patterns of hunters who use private land and those who use public land. We will find a national trend away from public land hunting over the last twenty years of the 20th Century. Private land hunters tended to specialize in private land use, whereas the majority of public land hunters hunted on private land as well.

Demographically, the single characteristic that most determined a hunter's use of private or public land was the region of the country he or she lived in; different parts of the country vary widely in the availability of public and private land. Private land hunters also tended to be more rural. Other demographic characteristics, such as age, race and ethnicity, income, and education levels, were similar for both private and public land hunters, so they appeared not to have much influence on what type of land was chosen. The primary characteristic that influenced the choice of land was the proximate availability of private and public land.

This report presents information in the following order: U.S. landownership overview, a summary of the trends of hunting on public and private land, average days of hunting by state, socioeconomic characteristics of public and private land hunters, expenditure patterns, land use by type of hunting, owning and leasing hunting land, and the valuation of the hunting experiences of public and private land hunters (i.e., willingness to pay more to hunt). The last section is a summary of findings.

Landownership Overview

The federal government owns three out of every ten acres of land in the U.S. There are 2.3 billion acres in the United States of which 672 million acres are owned by the federal government. State recreational areas, such as state parks, make up 13 million acres.[1] The extent of private land is more than twice that of public land. Of course, much of private land is not appropriate for hunting, e.g., urban areas. Also, not all public land is available for hunting, e.g., most national parks.

The availability of public land varies widely by region of the country. Most public land is in the West and therefore not easily accessible to the many large population areas in the East. The percentage extremes of federal land in different areas of the country are 2% in the Middle Atlantic region and 58% in the Pacific region. The two regions of the country that are dominated by federal land are the Pacific and Mountain (51%) regions. The rest of the country has single-digit percentages: New England (4%), West North Central (4%), West South Central (4%), East North Central (5%), East South Central (6%), and South Atlantic (9%). The state with the most federal land percentage-wise is Nevada (92%) and acreage-wise is Alaska (244 million acres).[2]

Figure 1. Extent of Federally Owned Land by Region

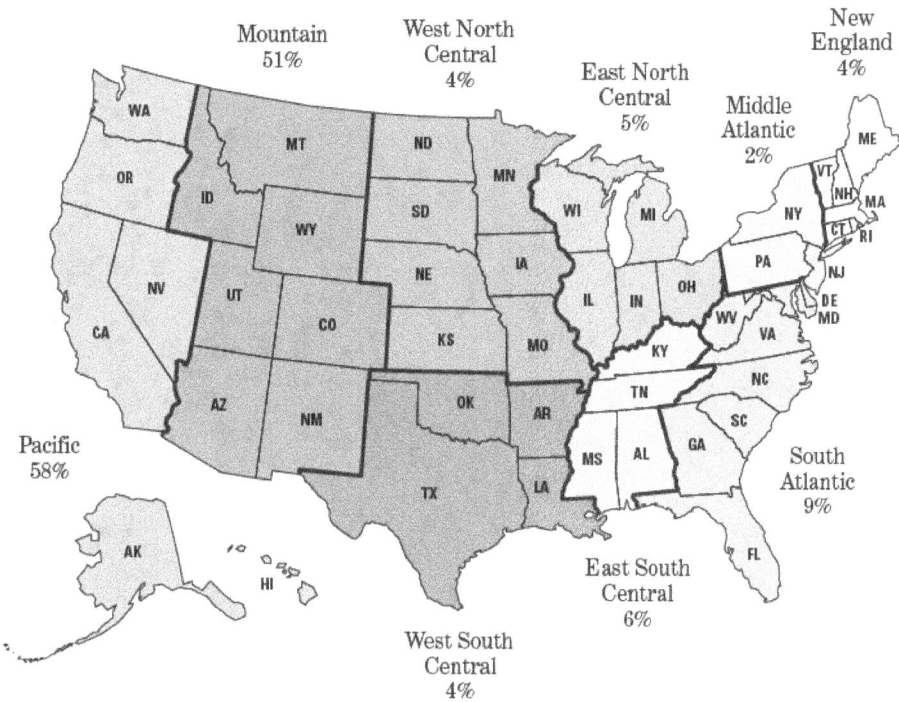

Source: *Statistical Abstract of the United States: 2004-2005, Table 347.*

The National Survey of Fishing, Hunting, and Wildlife-Associated Recreation provides estimates of the number of hunters who use public and private land and their days of hunting. Private land hunting is more prevalent than public land hunting both nationally and for most states. In 2001 82% of all hunters used private land and 40% of hunters used public land. (Some hunters used both public and private land, which explains why the sum of 82% and 40% is greater than 100%.) Forty-two states in 2001 had a majority of hunters hunt on private land. In fact, in thirteen states 90% or more of in-state hunters[3] hunted on private land. The eight states where the majority of hunters hunted on public land were in the Mountain and Pacific regions. See Appendix I for more state information.

In 2001 10.7 million hunters used private land. Texas (1,080,000), Pennsylvania (749,000), New York (636,000), and Michigan (595,000) had the most in-state hunters who used private land.

[1] Statistical Abstract of the United States: 2004-2005, tables 346, 347, and 1250. Issued 2004.

[2] Statistical Abstract of the United States: 2004-2005, table 347. Issued 2004.

[3] In-state hunters are all hunters, both state residents and nonresidents, hunting in a state.

Trends

For technical reasons (primarily changes in the respondent's recall period) the 1980 and 1985 National Survey estimates are not directly comparable to the 1991-2001 Survey estimates, but the proportions of totals can be compared. 45% of hunters hunted on public land in 1980 and 40% did in 2001. 32% of hunting days were on public land in 1980 and 26% were in 2001. In 27 states the percent of state resident hunters using public land declined from 1980 to 2001, and in 21 states it increased. These statistics indicate a trend away from public land hunting over the last twenty years of the 20th century. Part of the reason is that state fish and game agencies have begun to promote private land use. For example, Colorado, Kansas, Nebraska, North Dakota, and South Dakota have "Walk-in" hunting programs that provide public access to private land hunting.

From 1980 to 2001 small game, migratory bird, and other animal (nongame such as coyotes and groundhogs) hunters had little change in either public or private participation levels, while big game hunters shifted away from public land use. 47% of big game hunters hunted on public land in 1980, which compares to only 37% in 2001. Moreover, 41% of big game hunting days in 1980 were on public land, while 24% of big game hunting days were on public land in 2001.

Table 1. Trend in Public and Private Land Hunting, by Percent of Total Hunters

	1980	1985	1991	1996	2001
Public Land Hunter Percentage					
Total hunting	45	47	44	47	40
Big game	47	47	43	44	37
Small game	33	34	34	38	36
Migratory bird	32	32	29	36	35
Other animals	21	20	21	26	27
Private Land Hunter Percentage					
Total hunting	N.A.	82	83	81	82
Big game	N.A.	74	79	77	80
Small game	N.A.	82	84	82	80
Migratory bird	N.A.	76	82	77	76
Other animals	N.A.	85	90	86	86

Table 2. Big Game Private and Public Land Hunting
(Numbers in thousands.)

	1980		1985		1991		1996		2001	
	Number	Percent	Number	Percent	Number	Percent	Number	Percent	Number	Percent
Total hunters	N.A.	100	N.A.	100	10,745	100	11,288	100	10,911	100
Total public land hunters	N.A.	47	N.A.	47	4,626	43	4,937	44	3,998	37
Public land only hunters	N.A.	N.A.	N.A.	24	2,162	20	2,353	21	1,815	17
Public and private land hunters	N.A.	N.A.	N.A.	23	2,451	23	2,584	23	2,183	20
Total private land hunters	N.A.	N.A.	N.A.	74	8,464	79	8,746	77	8,748	80
Private land only hunters	N.A.	N.A.	N.A.	51	5,990	56	6,162	55	6,565	60
Public and private land hunters	N.A.	N.A.	N.A.	23	2,451	23	2,584	23	2,183	20
Total hunting days	N.A.	100	N.A.	100	128,411	100	153,784	100	153,191	100
Public land days	N.A.	41	N.A.	34	37,434	29	43,409	28	36,070	24
Private land days	N.A.	59	N.A.	68	90,432	70	105,627	69	110,283	72

Table 3. Small Game Private and Public Land Hunting
(Numbers in thousands.)

	1980		1985		1991		1996		2001	
	Number	Percent	Number	Percent	Number	Percent	Number	Percent	Number	Percent
Total hunters	N.A.	100	N.A.	100	7,642	100	6,945	100	5,434	100
Total public land hunters	N.A.	33	N.A.	34	2,634	34	2,655	38	1,972	36
Public land only hunters	N.A.	N.A.	N.A.	15	1,089	14	1,110	16	935	17
Public and private land hunters	N.A.	N.A.	N.A.	19	1,542	20	1,545	22	1,037	19
Total private land hunters	N.A.	N.A.	N.A.	82	6,424	84	5,713	82	4,345	80
Private land only hunters	N.A.	N.A.	N.A.	63	4,840	63	4,168	60	3,308	61
Public and private land hunters	N.A.	N.A.	N.A.	19	1,542	20	1,545	22	1,037	19
Total hunting days	N.A.	100	N.A.	100	77,132	100	75,117	100	60,142	100
Public land days	N.A.	26	N.A.	23	19,093	25	20,069	27	16,170	27
Private land days	N.A.	74	N.A.	75	57,391	74	54,993	73	42,382	70

USFWS/Mike Hemming

Table 4. Migratory Bird Private and Public Land Hunting
(Numbers in thousands.)

	1980		1985		1991		1996		2001	
	Number	*Percent*	*Number*	*Percent*	*Number*	*Percent*	*Number*	*Percent*	*Number*	*Percent*
Total hunters	N.A.	100	N.A.	100	3,009	100	3,073	100	2,956	100
Total public land hunters	N.A.	32	N.A.	32	887	29	1,117	36	1,045	35
Public land only hunters	N.A.	N.A.	N.A.	18	487	16	641	21	576	19
Public and private land hunters	N.A.	N.A.	N.A.	14	400	13	476	15	469	16
Total private land hunters	N.A.	N.A.	N.A.	76	2,454	82	2,377	77	2,255	76
Private land only hunters	N.A.	N.A.	N.A.	62	2,046	68	1,901	62	1,787	60
Public and private land hunters	N.A.	N.A.	N.A.	14	400	13	476	15	469	16
Total hunting days	N.A.	100	N.A.	100	22,235	100	26,501	100	29,310	100
Public land days	N.A.	29	N.A.	28	5,538	25	7,809	29	9,126	31
Private land days	N.A.	67	N.A.	68	15,512	70	17,674	67	19,707	67

Table 5. Other Animal Private and Public Land Hunting
(Numbers in thousands.)

	1980		1985		1991		1996		2001	
	Number	*Percent*	*Number*	*Percent*	*Number*	*Percent*	*Number*	*Percent*	*Number*	*Percent*
Total hunters	N.A.	100	N.A.	100	1,411	100	1,521	100	1,047	100
Total public land hunters	N.A.	21	N.A.	20	293	21	394	26	287	27
Public land only hunters	N.A.	N.A.	N.A.	10	124	9	155	10	104	10
Public and private land hunters	N.A.	N.A.	N.A.	10	168	12	240	16	184	18
Total private land hunters	N.A.	N.A.	N.A.	85	1,273	90	1,307	86	904	86
Private land only hunters	N.A.	N.A.	N.A.	74	1,099	78	1,068	70	720	69
Public and private land hunters	N.A.	N.A.	N.A.	10	168	12	240	16	184	18
Total hunting days	N.A.	100	N.A.	100	19,340	100	24,522	100	19,207	100
Public land days	N.A.	18	N.A.	16	2,642	14	5,731	23	3,227	17
Private land days	N.A.	82	N.A.	83	15,655	81	19,871	81	16,076	84

At the state level, the trend from 1991 to 2001 is one of reduced participation extremes: in 1991 22 states had 90% or more of in-state hunters hunting on private land compared to 13 in 2001. The principal source of the change was the arc of states from Iowa to Ohio, where the dominance of private land hunting lessened.

Nationally there was a 9% decrease in the number of private land hunters from 1991 to 2001. This is similar to the trend in overall hunting participation, which decreased 7% over the same time period. Nonetheless there were areas with increases in hunters who used private land. The states with the greatest percentage increases in private land hunters were Arkansas (57%), North Dakota (38%), and South Dakota (36%). The states with the greatest increase in the number of hunters using private land were Arkansas (+140,000), Minnesota (105,000), and Texas (70,000).

Figure 2. Private Land Use in 2001, by Proportion of Total Hunters

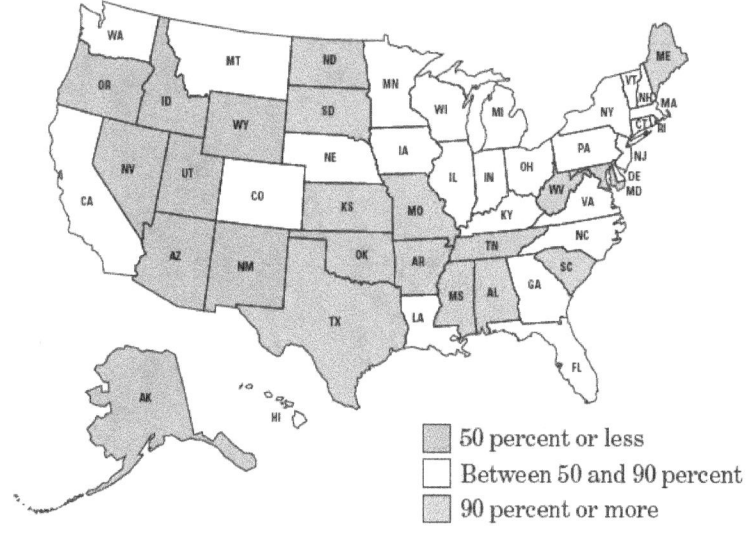

Figure 3. Private Land Use in 1996, by Proportion of Total Hunters

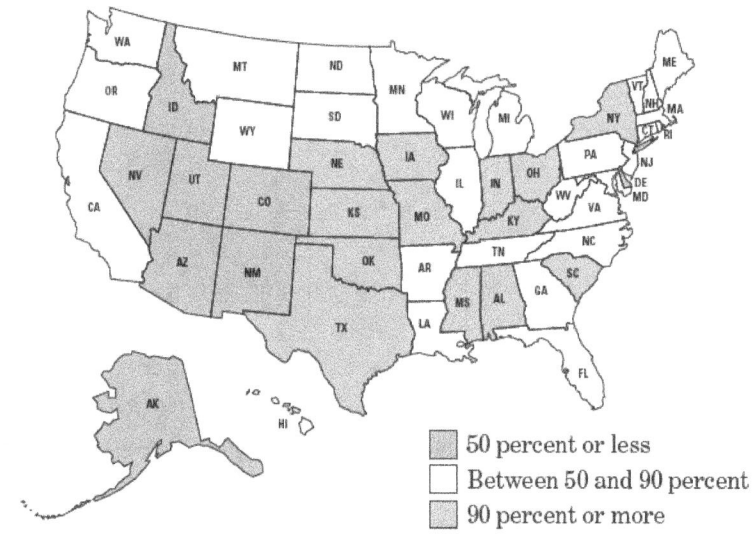

Figure 4. Private Land Use in 1991, by Proportion of Total Hunters

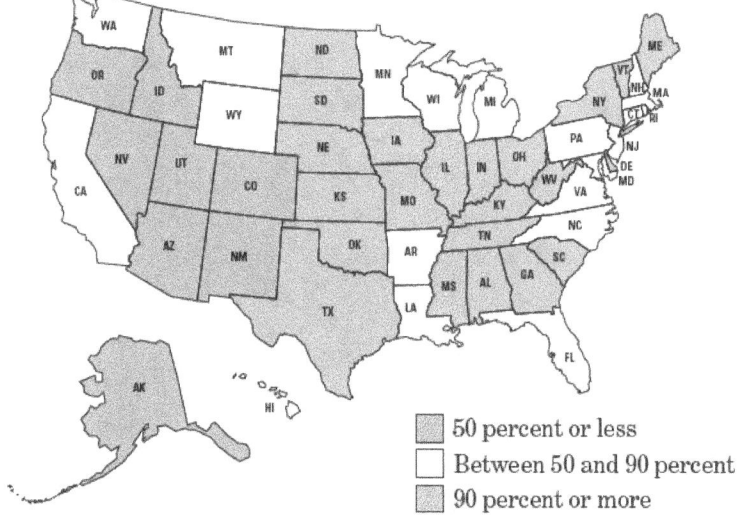

Table 6. 2001 Public and Private Land Hunters by State Where Hunting Took Place

(Numbers in thousands.)

	Total hunters	Public land hunters	Percent of total hunters	Private land hunters	Percent of total hunters	Public land only	Private land only	Public and Private land
Aggregate	**13,034**	**5,156**	**40**	**10,724**	**82**	**1,879**	**7,447**	**3,277**
Alabama	423	55	13	395	93	...	350	45
Alaska	93	85	91	18	19	72	*5	*13
Arizona	148	121	82	*47	*32	99	...	*23
Arkansas	431	156	36	386	90	*36	266	120
California	274	*122	*45	*178	*65	*69	*125	...
Colorado	281	194	69	160	57	120	87	73
Connecticut	45	*22	*49	*37	*82	...	*23	...
Delaware	16	*4	*25	14	88	...	*12	...
Florida	226	*104	*46	*141	*62	*77	*114	...
Georgia	417	*85	*20	373	89	...	298	*76
Hawaii	17	*10	*59	*11	*65	...	...	*6
Idaho	197	173	88	78	40	108	...	65
Illinois	310	*63	*20	269	87	...	236	...
Indiana	290	*83	*29	259	89	...	187	*72
Iowa	243	92	38	207	85	*32	147	61
Kansas	291	97	33	264	91	*24	191	73
Kentucky	323	76	24	289	90	...	232	*57
Louisiana	333	99	30	271	81	*41	213	*58
Maine	164	31	19	148	90	*13	130	*17
Maryland	145	*53	*37	131	90	...	90	*40
Massachusetts	66	43	65	48	73	*15	*20	*28
Michigan	754	248	33	595	79	*124	471	*124
Minnesota	597	262	44	482	81	*97	317	165
Mississippi	357	89	25	328	92	*20	260	69
Missouri	489	97	20	446	91	...	372	*74
Montana	229	156	68	132	58	91	67	65
Nebraska	173	53	31	150	87	*15	112	39
Nevada	47	45	96	*13	*28	33	...	*12
New Hampshire	78	33	42	65	83	*9	41	24
New Jersey	135	85	63	104	77	*20	*39	*65
New Mexico	130	122	94	*35	*27	95	...	*27
New York	714	252	35	636	89	*60	444	192
North Carolina	295	*90	*31	252	85	*34	196	*56
North Dakota	139	49	35	126	91	*12	90	37
Ohio	490	157	32	422	86	*48	312	110
Oklahoma	261	*79	*30	245	94	...	180	*65
Oregon	248	195	79	95	38	140	*40	55
Pennsylvania	1,000	484	48	749	75	209	475	275
Rhode Island	*9	*4	*44	*7	*78	...	...	...
South Carolina	265	53	20	243	92	*16	206	*37
South Dakota	209	79	38	182	87	*24	127	54
Tennessee	359	113	32	341	95	...	240	102
Texas	1,201	*189	*16	1,080	90	...	953	*127
Utah	198	170	86	86	43	110	*26	60
Vermont	100	47	47	81	81	*14	48	33
Virginia	355	115	32	309	87	*40	234	*75
Washington	227	160	71	128	56	93	60	68
West Virginia	284	70	25	262	92	*18	210	52
Wisconsin	660	240	36	577	87	*67	404	173
Wyoming	133	86	65	67	50	65	*46	21

Note: The Public land only, Private land only, and Public and Private land estimates may not add to Total hunters because some respondents did not answer the pertinent survey question or answered "don't know".

*Sample size between 10 and 30.

... Sample size less than 10.

Table 7. 1996 Public and Private Land Hunters by State Where Hunting Took Place
(Numbers in thousands.)

	Total hunters	Public land hunters	Percent of total hunters	Private land hunters	Percent of total hunters	Public land only	Private land only	Public and Private land
Aggregate	**13,975**	**6,533**	**47**	**11,383**	**82**	**2,344**	**7,195**	**4,188**
Alabama	347	100	29	329	95	...	247	83
Alaska	73	67	92	*18	*25	54	...	*13
Arizona	167	149	89	*37	*22	124	...	*26
Arkansas	379	150	40	335	88	*33	218	117
California	515	360	70	312	61	*198	*149	*162
Colorado	454	385	85	165	36	287	*68	97
Connecticut	62	33	53	43	69	*18	*28	*15
Delaware	40	12	30	36	90	*4	28	*8
Florida	*184	*68	*37	*139	*76	...	*109	...
Georgia	403	*111	*28	355	88	...	280	*75
Hawaii	23	*15	*65	*15	*65	*8	*8	*7
Idaho	248	210	85	113	46	133	*37	77
Illinois	432	*133	*31	379	88	*43	289	*90
Indiana	357	98	28	320	90	...	253	*66
Iowa	368	105	29	342	93	...	258	84
Kansas	275	*54	*20	262	95	...	217	*45
Kentucky	377	*61	*16	351	93	...	306	*46
Louisiana	352	142	40	269	76	*77	205	*64
Maine	195	51	26	168	86	*16	133	35
Maryland	160	71	44	118	74	*40	87	*31
Massachusetts	84	*43	*51	64	76	*20	*41	*23
Michigan	934	490	53	716	77	219	444	271
Minnesota	588	332	57	463	79	*120	252	211
Mississippi	433	116	27	397	92	*31	312	85
Missouri	552	192	35	510	92	*33	351	159
Montana	195	136	70	124	64	70	58	65
Nebraska	176	54	31	162	92	...	121	41
Nevada	52	46	89	*17	*33	35	...	*11
New Hampshire	84	41	49	65	77	*15	39	26
New Jersey	95	*40	*42	*68	*72	*27	*55	...
New Mexico	97	67	69	35	36	52	*20	*15
New York	642	231	36	594	93	*42	405	189
North Carolina	370	*128	*35	320	87	...	223	*97
North Dakota	88	39	44	70	80	*11	42	27
Ohio	479	203	42	436	91	...	270	166
Oklahoma	297	134	45	267	90	...	155	*112
Oregon	293	238	81	152	52	138	*52	100
Pennsylvania	879	521	59	660	75	208	347	312
Rhode Island	26	18	69	16	62	*11	*8	*8
South Carolina	300	82	27	277	92	...	213	64
South Dakota	186	71	38	163	88	*22	114	49
Tennessee	408	180	44	347	85	*56	223	124
Texas	911	*139	*15	822	90	...	745	...
Utah	143	126	88	53	37	89	*16	*37
Vermont	106	41	39	89	84	*14	63	26
Virginia	392	152	39	339	87	*40	227	112
Washington	271	211	78	161	59	105	*55	*106
West Virginia	369	122	33	313	85	*51	242	71
Wisconsin	665	302	45	590	89	*64	353	238
Wyoming	136	88	65	85	63	48	45	39

Note: The Public land only, Private land only, and Public and Private land estimates may not add to Total hunters because some respondents did not answer the pertinent survey question or answered "don't know".

*Sample size between 10 and 30.

... Sample size less than 10.

Table 8. 1991 Public and Private Land Hunters by State Where Hunting Took Place
(Numbers in thousands.)

	Total hunters	Public land hunters	Percent of total hunters	Private land hunters	Percent of total hunters	Public land only	Private land only	Public and Private land
Aggregate	**14,063**	**6,204**	**44**	**11,725**	**83**	**2,115**	**7,587**	**4,073**
Alabama	359	89	25	328	91	*30	269	59
Alaska	69	60	87	19	28	44	...	16
Arizona	182	144	79	54	30	104	*14	*40
Arkansas	314	148	47	246	78	61	159	87
California	446	234	53	286	64	135	187	99
Colorado	348	270	78	160	46	182	72	88
Connecticut	57	21	37	35	61	*8	22	*13
Delaware	26	9	35	24	92	...	17	7
Florida	253	106	42	189	75	*63	146	*43
Georgia	412	96	23	376	91	*34	314	62
Hawaii	18	11	61	13	72	*5	*7	*6
Idaho	198	168	87	79	41	107	*18	61
Illinois	449	139	31	407	91	*42	310	97
Indiana	331	99	30	303	92	*21	225	78
Iowa	328	82	25	312	95	*14	244	68
Kansas	241	56	23	224	93	*17	185	39
Kentucky	370	85	23	343	93	*22	280	63
Louisiana	332	121	36	293	88	*36	208	85
Maine	165	39	24	151	92	*11	123	28
Maryland	147	65	44	114	78	*25	74	40
Massachusetts	108	76	70	74	69	*31	29	45
Michigan	826	458	55	690	84	133	365	325
Minnesota	458	244	53	377	82	73	206	171
Mississippi	364	113	31	339	93	*19	245	94
Missouri	520	192	37	481	93	40	329	152
Montana	223	166	74	151	68	69	54	97
Nebraska	168	44	26	163	97	...	123	40
Nevada	57	51	90	24	42	33	...	18
New Hampshire	73	29	40	61	84	*10	42	19
New Jersey	135	73	54	85	63	*45	57	*28
New Mexico	109	92	84	35	32	73	*16	19
New York	742	294	40	670	90	*67	443	227
North Carolina	398	115	29	352	88	*33	270	82
North Dakota	98	47	48	91	93	*7	51	40
Ohio	615	173	28	570	93	*43	440	130
Oklahoma	244	76	31	220	90	*23	167	53
Oregon	253	197	78	114	45	132	49	65
Pennsylvania	1,027	604	59	811	79	208	415	396
Rhode Island	22	13	59	17	77	*5	*9	*8
South Carolina	235	54	23	215	92	*15	176	39
South Dakota	147	73	50	134	91	*13	74	60
Tennessee	361	115	32	328	91	*34	247	81
Texas	1,060	162	15	1,010	95	*50	898	112
Utah	177	149	84	75	42	99	*25	50
Vermont	101	43	43	92	91	*9	58	34
Virginia	402	142	35	358	89	*31	247	111
Washington	248	195	79	152	61	93	50	102
West Virginia	342	86	25	312	91	*27	253	59
Wisconsin	747	324	43	629	84	110	415	214
Wyoming	135	100	74	74	55	61	35	39

Note: The Public land only, Private land only, and Public and Private land estimates may not add to Total hunters because some respondents did not answer the pertinent survey question or answered "don't know".

*Sample size between 10 and 30.

... Sample size less than 10.

In terms of hunting days, there was no statistically significant change in hunting days nationally on private land in 2001 compared to 1991.[3] This is similar to the trend in overall hunting days, where the 3% decrease over the same time period is not statistically significant. Nonetheless there were states with increases in private land use. The states with the greatest percentage increase in private land hunting days were New Mexico (158%), Utah (123%), and Oklahoma (115%). The states with the greatest increase in the number of days were Oklahoma (+3.3 million), Arkansas (2.9 million), Alabama (2.6 million), and Georgia (2.5 million).

From 1991 to 2001 the number of public land hunters fell faster than the number of private land hunters. 17% fewer public land hunters hunted in 2001 compared to 1991, nearly twice the rate of decrease of the private land hunters. The only states with significant increases in the number of public land hunters were Kansas with a 73% increase (41,000), Alaska with a 42% increase (25,000), and New Mexico with a 33% increase (30,000).

Nationwide, the number of public land hunting days did not change from 1991 to 2001. In only one state was there a significant increase: Kansas, with a 199% increase (+0.6 million).

---

[3] The significance test was at the 95% level. This means that for 95% of all possible samples the estimate for 2001 cannot be shown to be different from the estimate for 1991.

Figure 5. Private Land Use in 2001, by Proportion of Total Hunting Days

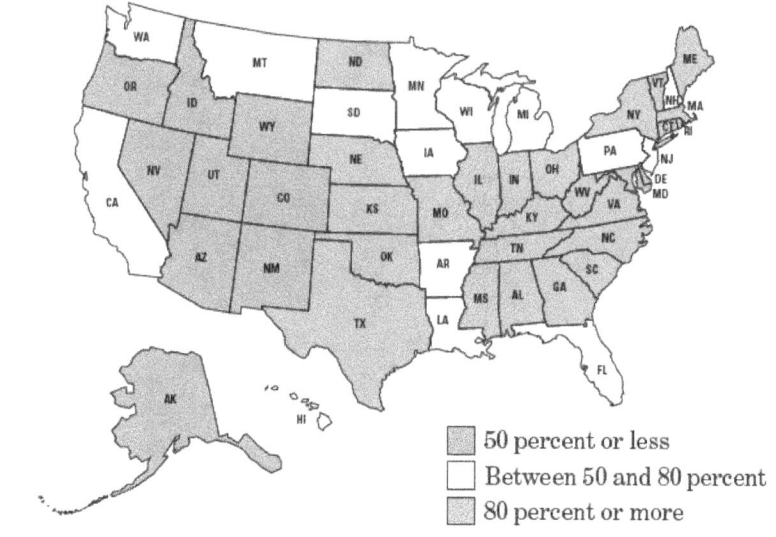

▨ 50 percent or less
☐ Between 50 and 80 percent
▨ 80 percent or more

Figure 6. Private Land Use in 1996, by Proportion of Total Hunting Days

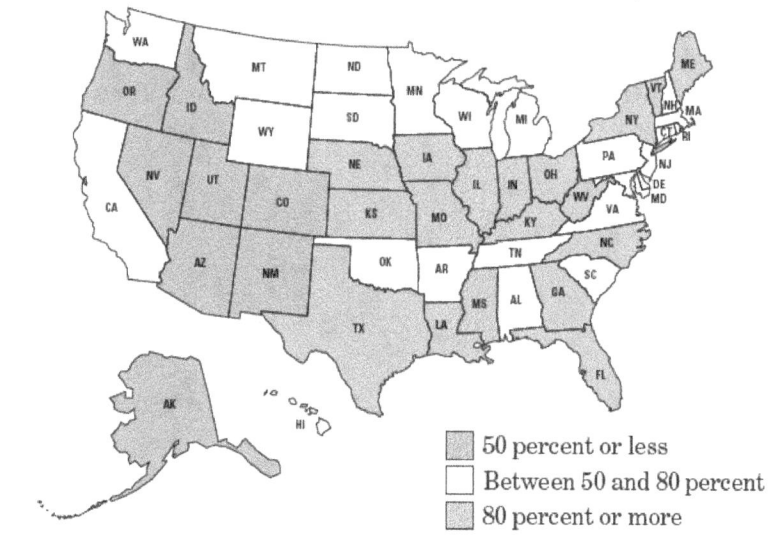

▨ 50 percent or less
☐ Between 50 and 80 percent
▨ 80 percent or more

Figure 7. Private Land Use in 1991, by Proportion of Total Hunting Days

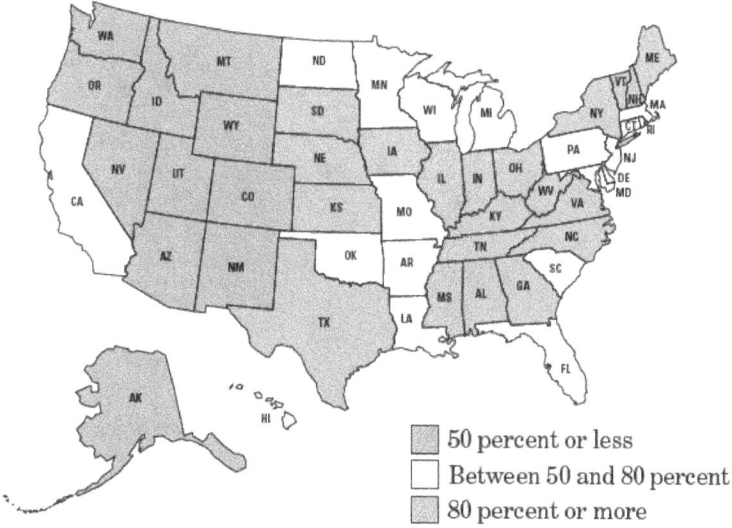

▨ 50 percent or less
☐ Between 50 and 80 percent
▨ 80 percent or more

Table 9. 2001 Public and Private Land Hunting Days by State Where Hunting Took Place
(Numbers in thousands.)

	Total days	Public land days	Percent of total days	Private land days	Percent of total days	Average hunting days	Average public land days	Average private land days
Aggregate	**228,368**	**64,592**	**28**	**188,448**	**83**	**18**	**13**	**18**
Alabama	7,616	426	6	7,416	97	18	8	19
Alaska	1,146	996	87	190	17	12	12	11
Arizona	1,694	1,414	84	*411	24	11	12	9
Arkansas	8,411	2,002	24	6,654	79	20	13	17
California	3,426	*1,697	50	*1,920	56	13	14	11
Colorado	2,610	1,650	63	1,259	48	9	9	8
Connecticut	766	*196	26	*647	84	17	9	17
Delaware	226	*60	27	186	82	14	15	13
Florida	4,693	*2,350	50	*2,732	58	21	23	19
Georgia	7,973	*927	12	7,446	93	19	11	20
Hawaii	316	*234	74	*181	57	19	23	16
Idaho	2,100	1,763	84	720	34	11	10	9
Illinois	4,522	*1,049	23	4,143	92	15	17	15
Indiana	5,000	*608	12	4,920	98	17	7	19
Iowa	3,989	1,232	31	3,055	77	16	13	15
Kansas	3,647	967	27	3,505	96	13	10	13
Kentucky	4,664	587	13	4,550	98	14	8	16
Louisiana	6,442	1,239	19	5,077	79	19	13	19
Maine	2,469	367	15	2,416	98	15	12	16
Maryland	1,799	*235	13	1,688	94	12	4	13
Massachusetts	1,158	*440	38	943	81	18	10	20
Michigan	8,994	3,352	37	6,513	72	12	14	11
Minnesota	8,437	2,813	33	5,381	64	14	11	11
Mississippi	8,481	1,590	19	7,859	93	24	18	24
Missouri	6,606	806	12	6,464	98	14	8	15
Montana	2,442	1,595	65	1,260	52	11	10	10
Nebraska	2,204	341	16	2,057	93	13	6	14
Nevada	490	446	91	*136	28	10	10	10
New Hampshire	1,459	315	22	1,111	76	19	10	17
New Jersey	3,120	1,190	38	1,884	60	23	14	18
New Mexico	1,667	1,589	95	*644	39	13	13	18
New York	13,187	4,423	34	12,407	94	19	18	20
North Carolina	7,526	*1,393	19	6,662	89	26	15	26
North Dakota	1,635	424	26	1,470	90	12	9	12
Ohio	10,233	1,306	13	8,966	88	21	8	21
Oklahoma	5,642	*1,155	20	5,642	100	22	15	23
Oregon	2,947	2,402	82	859	29	12	12	9
Pennsylvania	13,955	5,193	37	9,519	68	14	11	13
Rhode Island	104	*40	38	*91	88	12	10	13
South Carolina	4,744	650	14	4,402	93	18	12	18
South Dakota	2,425	698	29	1,700	70	12	7	8
Tennessee	6,651	1,537	23	6,475	97	19	14	19
Texas	14,081	*1,403	10	14,081	100	12	7	13
Utah	2,455	1,986	81	731	30	12	12	9
Vermont	1,510	399	26	1,223	81	15	9	15
Virginia	5,818	1,016	18	5,118	88	16	9	17
Washington	2,951	1,816	62	1,326	45	13	11	10
West Virginia	5,166	761	15	5,029	97	18	11	19
Wisconsin	9,653	2,493	26	7,214	75	15	10	13
Wyoming	1,304	960	74	580	45	10	11	9

Note: Total days is less than the sum of Public land days and Private land days because some days were spent on both public and private land.
*Sample size between 10 and 30.

Table 10. 1996 Public and Private Land Hunting Days by State Where Hunting Took Place
(Numbers in thousands.)

	Total days	Public land days	Percent of total days	Private land days	Percent of total days	Average hunting days	Average public land days	Average private land days
Aggregate	**256,676**	**77,018**	**30**	**198,165**	**77**	**18**	**12**	**17**
Alabama	7,181	1,226	17	5,619	78	21	12	17
Alaska	1,067	976	92	*245	23	15	15	14
Arizona	1,630	1,568	96	*248	15	10	11	7
Arkansas	8,381	2,692	32	5,969	71	22	18	18
California	7,452	3,512	47	4,307	58	15	10	14
Colorado	4,287	3,404	79	1,297	30	9	9	8
Connecticut	854	393	46	561	66	14	12	13
Delaware	716	271	38	533	74	18	23	15
Florida	*4,446	*673	15	*4,438	100	24	10	32
Georgia	6,993	*1,169	17	5,716	82	17	11	16
Hawaii	258	*176	68	*140	54	11	12	9
Idaho	3,301	2,839	86	1,233	37	13	14	11
Illinois	6,488	*892	14	5,936	92	15	7	16
Indiana	6,204	955	15	5,277	85	17	10	17
Iowa	5,182	819	16	4,878	94	14	8	14
Kansas	3,954	*362	9	3,954	100	14	7	15
Kentucky	5,454	*610	11	4,928	90	15	10	14
Louisiana	6,756	1,659	25	5,725	85	19	12	21
Maine	3,144	1,034	33	2,586	82	16	20	15
Maryland	1,741	649	37	1,274	73	11	9	11
Massachusetts	1,261	*625	50	841	67	15	15	13
Michigan	18,408	6,483	35	11,831	64	20	13	17
Minnesota	6,984	3,216	46	4,671	67	12	10	10
Mississippi	8,327	1,167	14	7,845	94	19	10	20
Missouri	8,508	2,189	26	6,966	82	15	11	14
Montana	1,807	1,162	64	1,131	63	9	9	9
Nebraska	2,264	358	16	2,103	93	13	7	13
Nevada	649	536	83	*123	19	13	12	7
New Hampshire	1,204	507	42	947	79	14	12	15
New Jersey	2,242	*501	22	*1,188	53	24	13	17
New Mexico	632	463	73	197	31	7	7	6
New York	11,552	2,067	18	10,043	87	18	9	17
North Carolina	7,834	*2,297	29	7,485	96	21	18	23
North Dakota	1,033	314	30	769	74	12	8	11
Ohio	7,933	2,178	28	7,841	99	17	11	18
Oklahoma	5,605	1,283	23	3,885	69	19	10	15
Oregon	4,281	2,707	63	1,575	37	15	11	10
Pennsylvania	13,173	5,025	38	9,257	70	15	10	14
Rhode Island	502	249	50	295	59	19	14	18
South Carolina	6,921	1,328	19	5,374	78	23	16	19
South Dakota	2,280	670	29	1,785	78	12	9	11
Tennessee	9,057	2,367	26	6,248	69	22	13	18
Texas	17,050	*1,229	7	17,050	100	19	9	21
Utah	1,660	1,321	80	279	17	12	11	5
Vermont	1,642	412	25	1,387	85	16	10	16
Virginia	7,470	1,904	26	4,840	65	19	13	14
Washington	4,732	2,718	57	2,934	62	18	13	18
West Virginia	6,262	1,216	19	5,466	87	17	10	18
Wisconsin	10,042	3,522	35	7,715	77	15	12	13
Wyoming	1,442	1,123	78	839	58	11	13	10

Note: Total days is less than the sum of Public land days and Private land days because some days were spent on both public and private land.
*Sample size between 10 and 30.

Table 11. 1991 Public and Private Land Hunting Days by State Where Hunting Took Place
(Numbers in thousands.)

	Total days	Public land days	Percent of total days	Private land days	Percent of total days	Average hunting days	Average public land days	Average private land days
Aggregate	**235,806**	**64,707**	**27**	**178,990**	**76**	**17**	**10**	**15**
Alabama	5,823	1,036	18	4,825	83	16	12	15
Alaska	847	697	82	159	19	12	12	8
Arizona	1,555	1,292	83	239	15	9	9	4
Arkansas	5,513	1,684	31	3,771	68	18	11	15
California	5,211	2,328	45	3,346	64	12	10	12
Colorado	2,644	1,814	69	1,061	40	8	7	7
Connecticut	840	242	29	615	73	15	12	18
Delaware	410	73	18	312	76	16	8	13
Florida	4,545	1,493	33	3,264	72	18	14	17
Georgia	5,905	1,024	17	4,917	83	14	11	13
Hawaii	245	119	49	130	53	14	11	10
Idaho	2,168	1,604	74	688	32	11	10	9
Illinois	6,863	1,032	15	5,993	87	15	7	15
Indiana	7,155	1,163	16	6,003	84	22	12	20
Iowa	4,005	693	17	3,567	89	12	9	11
Kansas	2,821	323	11	2,548	90	12	6	11
Kentucky	6,042	668	11	5,477	91	16	8	16
Louisiana	6,676	1,754	26	4,933	74	20	15	17
Maine	2,347	529	23	1,943	83	14	14	13
Maryland	2,276	607	27	1,672	74	16	9	15
Massachusetts	1,426	800	56	862	60	13	11	12
Michigan	15,088	5,508	37	10,584	70	18	12	15
Minnesota	5,235	2,357	45	3,808	73	11	10	10
Mississippi	8,607	1,575	18	7,295	85	24	14	22
Missouri	7,196	1,569	22	5,709	79	14	8	12
Montana	2,591	1,787	69	1,137	44	12	11	8
Nebraska	2,251	272	12	2,058	91	13	6	13
Nevada	565	440	78	164	29	10	9	7
New Hampshire	1,118	261	23	900	81	15	9	15
New Jersey	2,363	1,117	47	1,264	54	18	15	15
New Mexico	1,088	853	78	250	23	10	9	7
New York	13,110	3,240	25	10,851	83	18	11	16
North Carolina	6,849	975	14	5,581	82	17	9	16
North Dakota	1,297	391	30	1,020	79	13	8	11
Ohio	9,013	1,134	13	7,886	88	15	7	14
Oklahoma	3,676	662	18	2,910	79	15	9	13
Oregon	2,554	1,667	65	992	39	10	9	9
Pennsylvania	15,639	5,829	37	10,589	68	15	10	13
Rhode Island	350	166	47	210	60	16	13	12
South Carolina	3,945	700	18	3,086	78	17	13	14
South Dakota	1,878	578	31	1,504	80	13	8	11
Tennessee	7,315	1,024	14	6,059	83	20	9	19
Texas	15,028	1,340	9	14,077	94	14	8	14
Utah	1,354	1,117	83	328	24	8	8	4
Vermont	1,777	527	30	1,511	85	18	12	16
Virginia	8,728	1,591	18	7,193	82	22	11	20
Washington	3,386	2,220	66	1,459	43	14	11	10
West Virginia	6,104	616	10	5,311	87	18	7	17
Wisconsin	11,324	3,421	30	8,544	76	15	11	14
Wyoming	1,054	796	76	389	37	8	8	5

Note: Total days is usually less than the sum of Public land days and Private land days because some days were spent on both public and private land.

Average Days by State from 1991 to 2001

There are not only more private land hunters than public land hunters nationally, but on average private land hunters hunt more. In 2001 the average days for public land hunting was 13, and the average days for private land hunting was 18. There was an upward trend in average days for both public and private land hunting from 1991 to 2001. In 2001 the average days of public land hunting by state ranged from 4 (Maryland) to 23 (Florida and Hawaii). Average private land hunting days ranged from 8 (Colorado and South Dakota) to 26 (North Carolina). The mode (i.e., the single estimate that occurred most often) for average public land days was 10 (Idaho, Kansas, Massachusetts, Montana, Nevada, New Hampshire, Rhode Island,

and Wisconsin). The mode for average private land days was 13 (Delaware, Kansas, Maryland, Pennsylvania, Rhode Island, Texas, and Wisconsin).

In 1996 the average days for public land hunting was 12, and the average days for private land hunting was 17. Both averages were less than those for 2001. Average days of public land hunting by state ranged from 7 (Illinois, Kansas, Nebraska, and New Mexico) to 23 (Delaware). The range of average days for private land hunting was 5 (Utah) to 32 (Florida). The mode for average public land days was 10 (California, Florida, Indiana, Kentucky, Minnesota, Mississippi, Oklahoma, Pennsylvania, Utah, Vermont, and West Virginia). The mode for average private land days was

14 (Alaska, California, Iowa, Kentucky, Missouri, Pennsylvania, and Virginia).

In 1991 the average days for public land hunting was 10, and the average days for private land hunting was 15. Again, these averages are less than those for the next Survey (1996). The range of average days for public land hunting was 6 (Kansas and Nebraska) to 15 (New Jersey). The range of average days by state for private land hunting in 1991 was 4 (Arizona and Utah) to 22 (Mississippi). The mode for average public land days was 8 (Delaware, Iowa, Kentucky, Missouri, North Carolina, North Dakota, Oregon, South Dakota, Texas, Wyoming), and the mode for average private land days was 15 (Alabama, Arkansas, Illinois, Maryland, Michigan, New Hampshire, New Jersey).

PA Game Commission

Demographics

Demographics in 2001

The single characteristic that most determines a hunter's use of private or public land is the region of the country he or she lives in. The region with the highest public land usage was the Mountain region (85% of total hunters in the Mountain region used public land); the lowest was the West South Central (25%). 74% of Mountain hunting days were on public land, and 16% of hunting days in the South Central (both East and West) were. The region with the highest private land usage was the East South Central (95% of hunters in this region used private land!), and the lowest was the Mountain (43%). The East South Central region had the highest percent of hunting days on private land (85%); the Mountain region had the lowest percent (35%).

In 2001 40% of all hunters hunted on public land. Of all public land hunters, 50% lived in urban areas and 50% in rural areas. The age group with the highest public land hunting participation rate (43%) was the 55 to 64 year olds. The group with the lowest participation rate (32%) was the 65 and older participants. The income group with the highest participation rate was the $30,000 to $34,999 group (48%); the lowest was the less than $10,000 group (20%).

26% of all hunting days were on public land. 35% of urbanite hunter days were on public land, while 22% of ruralite hunter days were. Ruralite hunters rely on public land less than urbanite hunters.

82% of all hunters hunted on private land. Of all private land hunters, 42% came from urban areas and 58% from rural areas. The age group with the highest rate of private land hunting was the 25 to 34 year olds (85%) and the cohorts with the lowest rate were the 16 to 17 year olds and the 55 to 64 year olds, both at 80% (there was not much variation by age in private land use). The income group with the highest participation rate was $100,000 or more (87%), the lowest were the $10,000 to $19,999 and the $30,000 to $34,999 cohorts (75%).

Figure 8. Percent of Hunting Population that Hunts on Public Land by Region

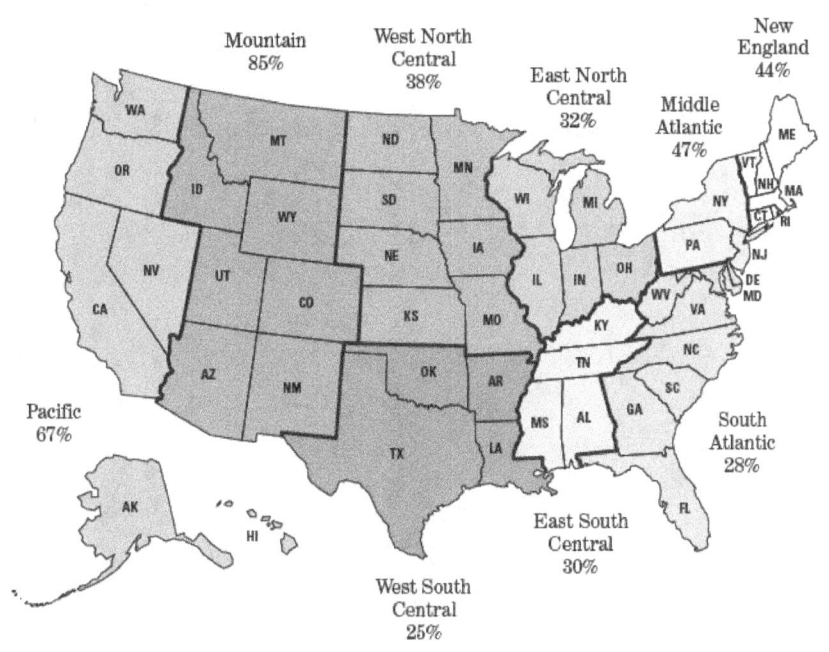

Figure 9. Percent of Hunting Population that Hunts on Private Land by Region

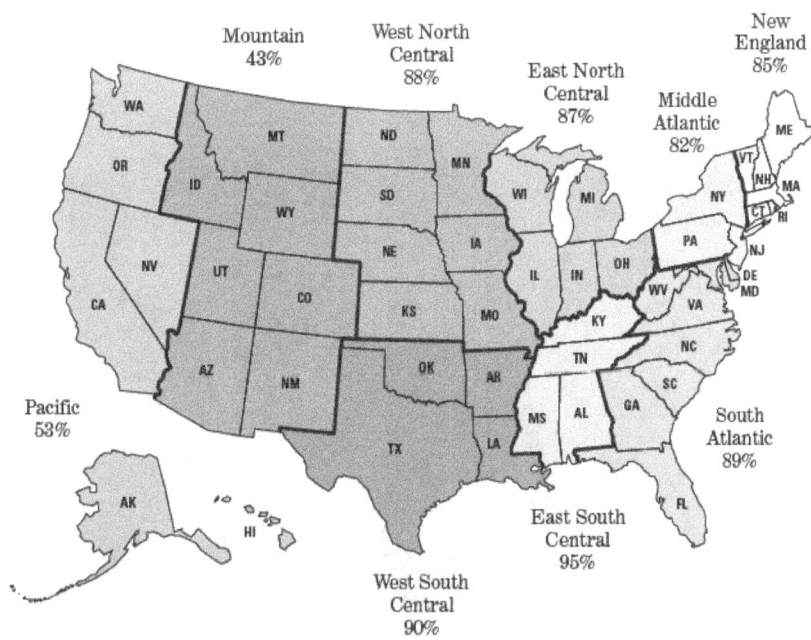

Table 12. Hunters and Days of Hunting on Public Land by Selected Characteristic: 2001
(Numbers in thousands.)

Characteristic	Total hunters, public and private land	Hunters on public land[1] Number	Percent of total hunters	Percent of hunters using public land	Total days, public and private land	Days on public land[2] Number	Percent of total days	Percent of days on public land
Total persons	**13,034**	**5,156**	**40**	**100**	**228,368**	**60,454**	**26**	**100**
Population Density of Residence								
Urban	5,873	2,592	44	50	84,455	29,225	35	48
Rural	7,161	2,564	36	50	143,913	31,229	22	52
Population Size of Residence								
Metropolitan statistical area (MSA)	7,749	3,177	41	62	121,857	34,888	29	58
1,000,000 or more	3,690	1,565	42	30	55,646	16,096	29	27
250,000 to 999,999	2,409	1,027	43	20	40,180	11,373	28	19
50,000 to 249,999	1,650	585	35	11	26,031	7,420	29	12
Outside MSA	5,285	1,978	37	38	106,511	25,566	24	42
Census Geographic Division								
New England	386	169	44	3	7,488	1,758	23	3
Middle Atlantic	1,633	761	47	15	30,060	9,538	32	16
East North Central	2,421	771	32	15	39,820	8,690	22	14
West North Central	1,710	655	38	13	27,186	7,109	26	12
South Atlantic	1,875	529	28	10	39,043	7,077	18	12
East South Central	1,164	349	30	7	25,482	4,156	16	7
West South Central	1,988	493	25	10	35,116	5,745	16	10
Mountain	1,020	871	85	17	12,995	9,641	74	16
Pacific	837	559	67	11	11,179	6,739	60	11
Age								
16 to 17 years	584	241	41	5	11,420	2,469	22	4
18 to 24 years	1,251	445	36	9	23,862	6,341	27	10
25 to 34 years	2,413	971	40	19	44,765	11,835	26	20
35 to 44 years	3,551	1,460	41	28	62,185	17,488	28	29
45 to 54 years	2,821	1,098	39	21	47,579	11,846	25	20
55 to 64 years	1,450	630	43	12	25,236	7,549	30	12
65 years and older	965	310	32	6	13,321	2,926	22	5
Sex								
Male	11,845	4,826	41	94	214,300	57,647	27	95
Female	1,190	329	28	6	14,068	2,808	20	5
Ethnicity								
Hispanic	428	205	48	4	5,139	2,027	39	3
Non-Hispanic	12,606	4,950	39	96	223,228	58,427	26	97
Race								
White	12,568	4,974	40	96	221,019	58,946	27	98
Black	297	95	32	2	5,383	706	13	1
Asian	*32	...	...	...	*332	...	...	...
All others	138	75	55	1	1,634	698	43	1

continues

Table 12. Hunters and Days of Hunting on Public Land by Selected Characteristic: 2001 – continued
(Numbers in thousands.)

| Characteristic | Total hunters, public and private land | Hunters on public land[1] | | | Total days, public and private land | Days on public land[2] | | |
		Number	Percent of total hunters	Percent of hunters using public land		Number	Percent of total days	Percent of days on public land
Annual Household Income								
Less than $10,000	247	50	20	1	4,525	553	12	1
$10,000 to $19,999	525	209	40	4	8,889	2,609	29	4
$20,000 to $24,999	565	194	34	4	10,747	2,820	26	5
$25,000 to $29,999	763	267	35	5	15,600	2,733	18	5
$30,000 to $34,999	830	398	48	8	14,532	5,222	36	9
$35,000 to $39,999	773	337	44	7	15,387	3,421	22	6
$40,000 to $49,999	1,569	632	40	12	26,000	7,185	28	12
$50,000 to $74,999	2,915	1,132	39	22	52,593	14,380	27	24
$75,000 to $99,999	1,525	689	45	13	25,935	8,088	31	13
$100,000 or more	1,267	522	41	10	17,879	4,644	26	8
Not reported	2,057	726	35	14	36,283	8,798	24	15
Education								
11 years or less	1,771	676	38	13	36,091	7,768	22	13
12 years	4,973	1,911	38	37	97,298	25,983	27	43
1 to 3 years college	3,412	1,379	40	27	53,206	15,434	29	26
4 years college	1,814	759	42	15	27,554	7,548	27	12
5 or more years college	1,065	430	40	8	14,219	3,721	26	6

* Estimate based on a small sample size.

… Sample size too small to report data reliably.

[1] Hunters on public land include those who hunted on both public and private land.

[2] Days of hunting on public land includes both days spent solely on public land and those spent on public and private land.

Note: Percent of total hunters and percent of total days are based on the total hunters and total days columns for each row. Percent of hunters using public land and percent of days on public land are based on the total number of hunters on public land and total number of days on public land, respectively.

74% of all hunting days were on private land. 65% of all urbanite hunting days were on private land, while 80% of all ruralite hunting days were. Interestingly, the age cohort with the lowest private land participation rate (16 to 17 years old's 80%) had the highest private land days participation rate (80%). Young people may not choose to hunt as much as older people, but when they do participate, they do it more than older people.

Differences in socioeconomic characteristics between public and private land hunters included a tendency of private land hunters to be more rural (58% of private land hunters lived in rural areas versus 50% of public land hunters). Also, private land hunters had slightly more activity by women (9%

of private land hunters were women compared to 6% of public land hunters). Overall, the age, race and ethnicity, income, and education profiles were remarkably similar for the private and public land hunters. The qualities that attracted hunters to public and private lands apparently had little to do with most demographic characteristics. The primary characteristic that influenced the choice of land was the proximate availability of private and public land.

It is interesting that in the three states that have roughly equal proportions of federal and nonfederal (i.e., private and state) land, Arizona, Oregon, and Wyoming, public land hunting is more prevalent than private land hunting. In 2001 in Arizona 82% of the hunters hunted on public land and 32% hunted

on private land. Similarly, in Oregon 79% hunted on public land and 38% hunted on private land. For Wyoming the percentages were 65% and 50%, respectively. Thus, there was not a preference for private land hunting when roughly equal amounts of public and private land were available.

Table 13. Hunters and Days of Hunting on Private Land by Selected Characteristic: 2001
(Numbers in thousands.)

| | | Hunters | | | | Days of hunting | | |
| | | Hunters on private land[1] | | | | Days on private land[2] | | |
Characteristic	Total hunters, public and private land	Number	Percent of total hunters	Percent of hunters using private land	Total days, public and private land	Number	Percent of total days	Percent of days on private land
Total persons	**13,034**	**10,724**	**82**	**100**	**228,368**	**169,795**	**74**	**100**
Population Density of Residence								
Urban	5,873	4,510	77	42	84,455	55,262	65	33
Rural	7,161	6,213	87	58	143,913	114,533	80	67
Population Size of Residence								
Metropolitan statistical area (MSA)	7,749	6,201	80	58	121,857	86,632	71	51
1,000,000 or more	3,690	2,835	77	26	55,646	38,278	69	23
250,000 to 999,999	2,409	1,964	82	18	40,180	29,310	73	17
50,000 to 249,999	1,650	1,401	85	13	26,031	19,043	73	11
Outside MSA	5,285	4,523	86	42	106,511	83,163	78	49
Census Geographic Division								
New England	386	326	85	3	7,488	5,871	78	3
Middle Atlantic	1,633	1,334	82	12	30,060	21,599	72	13
East North Central	2,421	2,111	87	20	39,820	30,142	76	18
West North Central	1,710	1,507	88	14	27,186	20,551	76	12
South Atlantic	1,875	1,669	89	16	39,043	32,012	82	19
East South Central	1,164	1,101	95	10	25,482	21,731	85	13
West South Central	1,988	1,790	90	17	35,116	28,702	82	17
Mountain	1,020	443	43	4	12,995	4,579	35	3
Pacific	837	444	53	4	11,179	4,608	41	3
Age								
16 to 17 years	584	468	80	4	11,420	9,145	80	5
18 to 24 years	1,251	1,041	83	10	23,862	18,323	77	11
25 to 34 years	2,413	2,047	85	19	44,765	33,186	74	20
35 to 44 years	3,551	2,890	81	27	62,185	45,072	72	27
45 to 54 years	2,821	2,311	82	22	47,579	35,631	75	21
55 to 64 years	1,450	1,166	80	11	25,236	18,170	72	11
65 years and older	965	801	83	7	13,321	10,267	77	6
Sex								
Male	11,845	9,766	82	91	214,300	158,552	74	93
Female	1,190	957	80	9	14,068	11,243	80	7
Ethnicity								
Hispanic	428	293	68	3	5,139	2,581	50	2
Non-Hispanic	12,606	10,431	83	97	223,228	167,213	75	98
Race								
White	12,568	10,377	83	97	221,019	164,095	74	97
Black	297	248	84	2	5,383	4,641	86	3
Asian	*32	...	...	...	*332	...	...	...
All others	138	80	58	1	1,634	924	57	1

continues

Table 13. Hunters and Days of Hunting on Private Land by Selected Characteristic: 2001 – continued
(Numbers in thousands.)

| | Hunters | | | | Days of hunting | | | |
| | | Hunters on private land[1] | | | | Days on private land[2] | | |
Characteristic	Total hunters, public and private land	Number	Percent of total hunters	Percent of hunters using private land	Total days, public and private land	Number	Percent of total days	Percent of days on private land
Annual Household Income								
Less than $10,000	247	203	82	2	4,525	3,806	84	2
$10,000 to $19,999	525	395	75	4	8,889	6,591	74	4
$20,000 to $24,999	565	471	83	4	10,747	7,963	74	5
$25,000 to $29,999	763	659	86	6	15,600	11,962	77	7
$30,000 to $34,999	830	624	75	6	14,532	9,427	65	6
$35,000 to $39,999	773	655	85	6	15,387	11,985	78	7
$40,000 to $49,999	1,569	1,252	80	12	26,000	18,762	72	11
$50,000 to $74,999	2,915	2,409	83	22	52,593	38,304	73	23
$75,000 to $99,999	1,525	1,221	80	11	25,935	18,776	72	11
$100,000 or more	1,267	1,103	87	10	17,879	13,215	74	8
Not reported	2,057	1,733	84	16	36,283	29,005	80	17
Education								
11 years or less	1,771	1,453	82	14	36,091	28,140	78	17
12 years	4,973	4,055	82	38	97,298	71,278	73	42
1 to 3 years college	3,412	2,752	81	26	53,206	38,875	73	23
4 years college	1,814	1,546	85	14	27,554	21,035	76	12
5 or more years college	1,065	917	86	9	14,219	10,467	74	6

* Estimate based on a small sample size.
… Sample size too small to report data reliably.
[1] Hunters on private land include those who hunted on both public and private land.
[2] Days of hunting on private land includes both days spent solely on private land and those spent on private and public land.
Note: Percent of total hunters and percent of total days are based on the total hunters and total days columns for each row. Percent of hunters using private land and percent of days on private land are based on the total number of hunters on private land and total number of days on private land, respectively.

Expenditures

1991–2001 Expenditures[4]

In 2001 private land hunters spent an average of $1,682 per spender (See Table 17). Spenders who hunted on both private and public land (31% of all private land spenders) were the biggest spenders, with an average of $2,452; they spent more for total trip-related, equipment, and other categories.

---

[4] All expenditure estimates in this report are in 2001 dollars.

Table 14. 2001 Expenditures for Hunting

	All hunters (thousands of dollars)	Average per hunter (dollars)	Private land only hunters (thousands of dollars)	Percent of total	Average per private land only hunter (dollars)	Private and public land hunter (thousands of dollars)	Percent of total	Average per private and public land hunter (dollars)	Public land only hunters (thousands of dollars)	Percent of total	Average per public land only hunter (dollars)
Total Expenditures	20,611,025	1,581	9,971,288	48	1,339	8,031,509	39	2,451	2,438,194	12	1,298
Total trip-related	5,252,391	403	2,120,315	40	285	2,463,074	47	752	592,002	11	315
Total equipment	10,361,496	795	5,514,889	53	741	3,546,192	34	1,082	1,237,729	12	659
Total hunting equipment[1]	4,561,709	350	2,127,887	47	286	1,858,014	41	567	534,503	12	285
Total auxiliary equipment[2]	1,202,845	92	500,303	42	67	491,153	41	150	193,958	16	103
Total special equipment[3]	4,596,942	353	2,886,699	63	388	1,197,025	26	365	509,269	11	271
Total other	4,997,138	383	2,336,084	47	314	2,022,243	41	617	608,463	12	324
Magazines, books	84,530	6	34,698	41	5	35,595	42	11	13,901	16	7
Membership dues and contributions	243,678	19	103,933	43	14	112,083	46	34	24,907	10	13
Land leasing and ownership	3,975,892	305	1,898,239	48	255	1,575,901	40	481	473,175	12	252
Ownership	3,351,389	257	1,449,961	43	195	1,431,366	43	437	459,155	14	244
Leasing	624,503	48	448,278	72	60	144,535	23	44	*14,020	*2	*7
Total licenses, stamps, tags, and permits	693,038	53	299,214	43	40	298,664	43	91	96,480	14	51
Licenses	572,242	44	257,449	45	35	242,373	42	74	74,718	13	40
Federal duck stamps	29,524	2	13,037	44	2	12,868	44	4	3,249	11	2
Other stamps, tags, and permits	91,273	7	28,728	32	4	43,423	48	13	18,513	20	10

[1] Includes rifles, shotguns, ammunition, archery equipment, hunting dogs, etc.

[2] Includes camping equipment, binoculars, special clothing, taxidermy costs, etc.

[3] Includes boats, boat accessories, pickups, campers, cabins, 4-wheelers, etc.

* Based on a sample size of 10.

Table 15. 1996 Expenditures for Hunting
(In 2001 dollars.)

	All hunters (thousands of dollars)	Average per hunter (dollars)	Private land only hunters (thousands of dollars)	Percent of total	Average per private land only hunter (dollars)	Private and public land hunter (thousands of dollars)	Percent of total	Average per private and public land hunter (dollars)	Public land only hunters (thousands of dollars)	Percent of total	Average per public land only hunter (dollars)
Total Expenditures	23,293,156	1,667	9,383,727	40	1,304	10,755,338	46	2,568	3,039,176	13	1,297
Total trip-related	5,825,511	417	2,113,601	36	294	2,920,999	50	698	759,805	13	324
Total equipment	12,738,229	912	4,555,536	36	633	6,166,463	48	1,472	1,930,848	15	824
Total hunting equipment	6,236,625	446	2,504,470	40	348	3,000,306	48	716	694,097	11	296
Total auxiliary equipment	1,393,423	99	518,659	37	72	677,556	49	162	184,728	13	79
Total special equipment	5,108,181	365	1,532,409	30	213	2,488,601	49	594	1,052,024	21	449
Total other	4,729,416	338	2,714,589	57	377	1,667,876	35	398	348,525	7	149
Magazines, books	123,923	9	48,306	39	7	62,344	50	15	12,906	10	6
Membership dues and contributions	276,743	20	97,858	35	14	155,519	56	37	22,922	8	10
Land leasing and ownership	3,592,197	257	2,285,364	64	318	1,114,731	31	266	*186,648	*5	*80
Ownership	N.A.	N.A.	N.A.	N.A.	N.A.	N.A.	N.A.	N.A.	N.A.	N.A.	N.A.
Leasing	N.A.	N.A.	N.A.	N.A.	N.A.	N.A.	N.A.	N.A.	N.A.	N.A.	N.A.
Total licenses, stamps, tags, and permits	736,554	53	283,061	38	39	335,281	46	80	126,049	17	54
Licenses	540,077	38	220,727	41	31	242,932	45	58	86,790	16	37
Federal duck stamps	34,903	2	13,532	39	2	16,356	47	4	4,664	13	2
Other stamps, tags, and permits	161,574	11	48,802	30	7	75,994	47	18	34,597	21	15

* Based on a sample size of 26.

Table 16. 1991 Expenditures for Hunting
(In 2001 dollars.)

	All hunters (thousands of dollars)	Average per hunter (dollars)	Private land only hunters (thousands of dollars)	Percent of total	Average per private land only hunter (dollars)	Private and public land hunter (thousands of dollars)	Percent of total	Average per private and public land hunter (dollars)	Public land only hunters (thousands of dollars)	Percent of total	Average per public land only hunter (dollars)
Total Expenditures	16,037,366	1,140	8,052,234	50	1,061	6,619,557	41	1,625	1,348,318	8	638
Total trip-related	4,472,785	319	1,662,140	37	219	2,291,402	51	563	507,330	11	240
Total equipment	6,719,081	478	3,077,125	46	406	2,924,086	44	718	684,523	10	324
Total hunting equipment[1]	4,268,437	303	1,825,846	43	241	2,034,026	48	499	397,188	9	188
Total auxiliary equipment[2]	825,934	59	312,248	38	41	413,629	50	102	98,605	12	47
Total special equipment[3]	1,624,710	116	939,032	58	124	476,432	29	117	188,730	12	89
Total other	4,845,499	345	3,312,969	68	437	1,404,069	29	345	156,465	3	74
Magazines, books	54,460	4	23,102	42	3	25,887	48	6	5,426	10	3
Membership dues and contributions	180,513	13	90,659	50	12	74,200	41	18	15,374	9	7
Land leasing and ownership	3,917,956	278	2,905,218	74	383	975,538	25	240	35,252	1	17
Ownership	3,508,055	250	2,620,172	75	345	866,609	25	213	**21,269	**1	10
Leasing	409,902	29	285,046	70	38	108,930	27	27	*13,983	*3	7
Total licenses, stamps, tags, and permits	692,571	49	293,989	42	39	328,444	47	81	100,413	15	48
Licenses	526,856	38	228,014	43	30	249,880	47	61	79,719	15	38
Federal duck stamps	28,428	3	11,757	41	2	13,902	49	3	2,675	9	1
Other stamps, tags, and permits	137,287	10	54,218	40	7	64,661	47	16	18,019	13	9

[1] Includes rifles, shotguns, ammunition, archery equipment, hunting dogs, etc.
[2] Includes camping equipment, binoculars, special clothing, taxidermy costs, etc.
[3] Includes boats, boat accessories, pickups, campers, cabins, 4-wheelers, etc.
* Based on a sample size of 21.
** Based on a sample size of 24.

Table 17. 2001 Expenditures by Private Land Use Hunters

	Private land hunters (thousands of dollars)	Number of spenders (thousands)	Average per spender (dollars)	Private land only hunters (thousands of dollars)	Number of spenders (thousands)	Average per spender (dollars)	Private and public land hunter (thousands of dollars)	Number of spenders (thousands)	Average per spender (dollars)
Total Expenditures	18,002,797	10,703	1,682	9,971,288	7,430	1,342	8,031,509	3,276	2,452
Total trip-related	4,583,390	10,709	428	2,120,315	7,440	285	2,463,074	3,271	753
Total equipment	9,061,081	8,406	1,078	5,514,889	5,532	997	3,546,192	2,876	1,233
Total hunting equipment[1]	3,985,901	8,052	495	2,127,887	5,241	406	1,858,014	2,811	661
Total auxiliary equipment[2]	991,456	3,843	258	500,303	2,349	213	491,153	1,497	328
Total special equipment[3]	4,083,724	497	8,222	2,886,699	314	9,205	1,197,025	183	6,538
Total other	4,358,326	9,099	479	2,336,084	6,068	385	2,022,243	3,023	669
Magazines, books	70,293	1,562	45	34,698	913	38	35,595	672	53
Membership dues and contributions	216,016	1,756	123	103,933	912	114	112,083	849	132
Land leasing and ownership	3,474,140	1,645	2,112	1,898,239	1,121	1,693	1,575,901	524	3,008
Ownership	2,881,327	869	3,317	1,449,961	571	2,538	1,431,366	297	4,815
Leasing	592,813	885	670	448,278	611	734	144,535	273	529
Total licenses, stamps, tags, and permits	597,877	8,665	69	299,214	5,754	52	298,664	2,928	102
Licenses	499,821	8,330	60	257,449	5,597	46	242,373	2,786	87
Federal duck stamps	25,905	1,727	15	13,037	869	15	12,868	858	15
Other stamps, tags, and permits	72,151	2,328	31	28,728	1,149	25	43,423	1,174	37

[1] Includes rifles, shotguns, ammunition, archery equipment, hunting dogs, etc.
[2] Includes camping equipment, binoculars, special clothing, taxidermy costs, etc.
[3] Includes boats, boat accessories, pickups, campers, cabins, 4-wheelers, etc.

Table 18. 1996 Expenditures by Private Land Use Hunters
(In 2001 dollars.)

	Private land hunters (thousands of dollars)	Number of spenders (thousands)	Average per spender (dollars)	Private land only hunters (thousands of dollars)	Number of spenders (thousands)	Average per spender (dollars)	Private and public land hunter (thousands of dollars)	Number of spenders (thousands)	Average per spender (dollars)
Total Expenditures	20,139,063	11,381	1,770	9,383,727	7,190	1,305	10,755,338	4,186	2,570
Total trip-related	5,034,600	11,366	443	2,113,601	7,166	295	2,920,999	4,176	700
Total equipment	10,721,999	9,682	1,107	4,555,536	5,868	776	6,166,463	3,814	1,617
Total hunting equipment[1]	5,504,776	9,386	587	2,504,470	5,654	443	3,000,306	3,724	806
Total auxiliary equipment[2]	1,196,215	4,878	245	518,659	2,608	199	677,556	2,263	299
Total special equipment[3]	4,021,009	644	6,240	1,532,409	332	4,616	2,488,601	313	7,964
Total other	4,382,464	9,919	442	2,714,589	5,946	457	1,667,876	3,978	419
Magazines, books	110,651	2,226	50	48,306	1,069	45	62,344	1,149	54
Membership dues and contributions	253,375	2,115	120	97,858	995	98	155,519	1,128	138
Land leasing and ownership	3,400,095	1,334	2,549	2,285,364	809	2,825	1,114,731	525	2,124
Ownership	N.A.	N.A.	N.A.	N.A.	N.A.	N.A.	N.A.	N.A.	N.A.
Leasing	N.A.	N.A.	N.A.	N.A.	N.A.	N.A.	N.A.	N.A.	N.A.
Total licenses, stamps, tags, and permits	618,343	9,435	66	283,061	5,693	50	335,281	3,804	88
Licenses	463,659	9,118	51	220,727	5,426	41	242,932	3,707	66
Federal duck stamps	29,887	1,763	17	13,532	798	17	16,356	965	17
Other stamps, tags, and permits	124,796	3,808	33	48,802	1,878	26	75,994	1,922	40

[1] Includes rifles, shotguns, ammunition, archery equipment, hunting dogs, etc.
[2] Includes camping equipment, binoculars, special clothing, taxidermy costs, etc.
[3] Includes boats, boat accessories, pickups, campers, cabins, 4-wheelers, etc.

Table 19. 1991 Expenditures by Private Land Use Hunters
(In 2001 dollars.)

	Private land hunters (thousands of dollars)	Number of spenders (thousands)	Average per spender (dollars)	Private land only hunters (thousands of dollars)	Number of spenders (thousands)	Average per spender (dollars)	Private and public land hunter (thousands of dollars)	Number of spenders (thousands)	Average per spender (dollars)
Total Expenditures	**14,671,791**	**11,720**	**1,252**	**8,052,234**	**7,647**	**1,053**	**6,619,557**	**4,074**	**1,625**
Total trip-related	3,953,542	11,697	338	1,662,140	7,611	218	2,291,402	4,071	563
Total equipment	6,001,212	9,499	632	3,077,125	5,830	528	2,924,086	3,669	797
Total hunting equipment[1]	3,859,872	9,192	420	1,825,846	5,618	325	2,034,026	3,572	569
Total auxiliary equipment[2]	725,877	3,650	199	312,248	1,937	161	413,629	1,711	242
Total special equipment[3]	1,415,463	405	3,497	939,032	214	4,399	476,432	191	2,490
Total other	4,717,038	10,279	459	3,312,969	6,387	519	1,404,069	3,899	360
Magazines, books	48,989	1,396	35	23,102	711	33	25,887	664	39
Membership dues and contributions	164,860	1,364	121	90,659	646	140	74,200	714	104
Land leasing and ownership	3,880,756	1,557	2,492	2,905,218	967	3,004	975,538	590	1,652
Ownership	3,486,781	726	4,802	2,620,172	392	6,683	866,609	334	2,595
Leasing	393,975	897	439	285,046	607	469	108,930	290	376
Total licenses, stamps, tags, and permits	622,432	9,975	62	293,989	6,282	47	328,444	3,887	85
Licenses	477,893	9,935	48	228,014	6,048	38	249,880	3,844	65
Federal duck stamps	25,659	1,316	20	11,757	603	20	13,902	713	20
Other stamps, tags, and permits	118,880	3,976	30	54,218	2,085	26	64,661	1,913	34

[1] Includes rifles, shotguns, ammunition, archery equipment, hunting dogs, etc.
[2] Includes camping equipment, binoculars, special clothing, taxidermy costs, etc.
[3] Includes boats, boat accessories, pickups, campers, cabins, 4-wheelers, etc.

USFWS/Kent Olson

Public land hunters spent an average of $2,032 per spender,[4] more than the average private land spender. However, the public-land-only[5] spender spent the lowest of any group, $1,298. It was the public and private land spender, 64% of all public land spenders, who was responsible for the high public land spender's average.

Private-land-only hunters and public-land-only hunters are similar in their spending patterns in all categories except land leasing costs. Public-land-only hunters spend much less on land leasing than private-land-only hunters. People who hunt on both public and private land spend on average nearly twice as much across all categories than do private-land-only and public-land-only hunters. People who hunt on both private and public land are perhaps more avid on average than hunters who hunt on public land only and private land only.

In 2001 1,645,000 private land hunters spent money on their owned or leased hunting land (869,000 owned land, 885,000 leased land), while 630,000 public land hunters spent money on their owned or leased land (366,000 owned land, 314,000 leased land). The great majority (83%) of the public land hunters that owned or leased land hunted on private land, as one would expect. Looking at the trend of leasing and owning over time, in 1991 owning and leasing costs by hunters totaled $3.9 billion by 1,659,000 spenders, averaging $2,362. In 1996 it totaled $3.6 billion by 1,443,000 spenders, averaging $2,489. Lastly, in 2001 it totaled $4.0 billion by 1,680,000 spenders, averaging $2,367. In short, a similar amount was spent in 1991 and 2001, with a drop in the expenditure total and spenders in 1996.

Interestingly, 83% of public land spenders spent money on hunting licenses, while slightly less, 78%, of private land spenders did (79% of all spenders purchased licenses). Given the landowner exemption (in some states landowners are exempt from being required to purchase a hunting license when they hunt on their own land), one would expect the lowest percentage of license purchasers would be private-land-only spenders. Their percentage was 75%. Similarly, the highest percentage would be expected to be public-land-only spenders. Theirs was 80%. The highest percentage was actually the public and private land spenders, 85%. Apparently their motivation to purchase a license was stronger because they engage in relatively more hunting.

Total land access fees by private land hunters totalled $411 million (74% of that total was for big game hunting), and by public land hunters $163 million (69% for big game hunting).

---

[4] Spenders are hunters who made hunting-related expenditures. Hunters who did not purchase anything are not included in the spender group.

[5] Public land hunters are every hunter who hunted on public land at least one day, and public-land-only hunters are people who did all their hunting on public land. A similar distinction is made for private land and private-land-only hunters. Public-land-only hunters are examined separately from public land hunters due to their strong reliance on public land.

Table 20. 2001 Expenditures by Public Land Use Hunters

	Public land hunters (thousands of dollars)	Number of spenders (thousands)	Average per spender (dollars)	Public land only hunters (thousands of dollars)	Number of spenders (thousands)	Average per spender (dollars)	Private and public land hunter (thousands of dollars)	Number of spenders (thousands)	Average per spender (dollars)
Total Expenditures	**10,469,703**	**5,152**	**2,032**	**2,438,194**	**1,878**	**1,298**	**8,031,509**	**3,276**	**2,452**
Total trip-related	3,055,077	5,143	594	592,002	1,879	315	2,463,074	3,271	753
Total equipment	4,783,921	4,294	1,114	1,237,729	1,416	874	3,546,192	2,876	1,233
Total hunting equipment[1]	2,392,517	4,118	581	534,503	1,310	408	1,858,014	2,811	661
Total auxiliary equipment[2]	685,111	2,168	316	193,958	671	289	491,153	1,497	328
Total special equipment[3]	1,706,294	252	6,769	509,269	69	7,382	1,197,025	183	6,538
Total other	2,630,707	4,632	568	608,463	1,614	377	2,022,243	3,023	669
Magazines, books	49,496	952	52	13,901	284	49	35,595	672	53
Membership dues and contributions	136,990	1,132	121	24,907	280	89	112,083	849	132
Land leasing and ownership	2,049,077	630	3,255	473,175	106	4,479	1,575,901	524	3,008
Ownership	1,890,522	366	5,167	459,155	69	6,693	1,431,366	297	4,815
Leasing	158,555	314	505	*14,020	*41	*346	144,535	273	529
Total licenses, stamps, tags, and permits	395,144	4,490	88	96,480	1,556	62	298,664	2,928	102
Licenses	317,091	4,285	74	74,718	1,494	50	242,373	2,786	87
Federal duck stamps	16,117	1,075	15	3,249	217	15	12,868	858	15
Other stamps, tags, and permits	61,936	1,770	35	18,513	561	33	43,423	1,174	37

[1] Includes rifles, shotguns, ammunition, archery equipment, hunting dogs, etc.
[2] Includes camping equipment, binoculars, special clothing, taxidermy costs, etc.
[3] Includes boats, boat accessories, pickups, campers, cabins, 4-wheelers, etc.
* Based on a sample size of 10.

Table 21. 1996 Expenditures by Public Land Use Hunters
(In 2001 dollars.)

	Public land hunters (thousands of dollars)	Number of spenders (thousands)	Average per spender (dollars)	Public land only hunters (thousands of dollars)	Number of spenders (thousands)	Average per spender (dollars)	Private and public land hunter (thousands of dollars)	Number of spenders (thousands)	Average per spender (dollars)
Total Expenditures	**13,794,512**	**6,525**	**2,114**	**3,039,176**	**2,339**	**1,300**	**10,755,338**	**4,186**	**2,570**
Total trip-related	3,680,801	6,515	565	759,805	2,335	325	2,920,999	4,176	700
Total equipment	8,097,311	5,701	1,420	1,930,848	1,886	1,024	6,166,463	3,814	1,617
Total hunting equipment[1]	3,694,403	5,504	671	694,097	1,780	390	3,000,306	3,724	806
Total auxiliary equipment[2]	862,284	3,077	280	184,728	813	227	677,556	2,263	299
Total special equipment[3]	3,540,625	463	7,656	1,052,024	150	7,013	2,488,601	313	7,964
Total other	2,016,400	6,070	332	348,525	2,084	167	1,667,876	3,978	419
Magazines, books	75,250	1,480	51	12,906	336	38	62,344	1,149	54
Membership dues and contributions	178,441	1,423	125	22,922	298	77	155,519	1,128	138
Land leasing and ownership	1,301,379	621	2,095	*186,648	*96	*1,939	1,114,731	525	2,124
Ownership	N.A.	N.A.	N.A.	N.A.	N.A.	N.A.	N.A.	N.A.	N.A.
Leasing	N.A.	N.A.	N.A.	N.A.	N.A.	N.A.	N.A.	N.A.	N.A.
Total licenses, stamps, tags, and permits	461,330	5,917	78	126,049	2,066	61	335,281	3,804	88
Licenses	329,722	5,721	58	86,790	1,969	44	242,932	3,707	66
Federal duck stamps	21,019	1,240	17	4,664	275	17	16,356	965	17
Other stamps, tags, and permits	110,590	2,796	40	34,597	851	41	75,994	1,922	40

[1] Includes rifles, shotguns, ammunition, archery equipment, hunting dogs, etc.
[2] Includes camping equipment, binoculars, special clothing, taxidermy costs, etc.
[3] Includes boats, boat accessories, pickups, campers, cabins, 4-wheelers, etc.
* Based on a sample size of 26.

Table 22. 1991 Expenditures by Public Land Use Hunters
(In 2001 dollars.)

	Public land hunters (thousands of dollars)	Number of spenders (thousands)	Average per spender (dollars)	Public land only hunters (thousands of dollars)	Number of spenders (thousands)	Average per spender (dollars)	Private and public land hunter (thousands of dollars)	Number of spenders (thousands)	Average per spender (dollars)
Total Expenditures	**7,967,876**	**6,204**	**1,284**	**1,348,318**	**2,130**	**633**	**6,619,557**	**4,074**	**1,625**
Total trip-related	2,798,732	6,186	452	507,330	2,121	239	2,291,402	4,071	563
Total equipment	3,608,609	5,228	690	684,523	1,553	441	2,924,086	3,669	797
Total hunting equipment[1]	2,431,213	5,041	482	397,188	1,469	270	2,034,026	3,572	569
Total auxiliary equipment[2]	512,233	2,332	220	98,605	627	157	413,629	1,711	242
Total special equipment[3]	665,163	263	2,534	188,730	71	2,653	476,432	191	2,490
Total other	1,560,534	5,827	268	156,465	1,910	82	1,404,069	3,899	360
Magazines, books	31,313	860	36	5,426	199	27	25,887	664	39
Membership dues and contributions	89,574	931	96	15,374	223	69	74,200	714	104
Land leasing and ownership	1,010,790	676	1,496	35,252	85	413	975,538	590	1,652
Ownership	887,878	374	2,373	**21,269	**40	**529	866,609	334	2,595
Leasing	122,914	340	361	*13,983	*50	*280	108,930	290	376
Total licenses, stamps, tags, and permits	428,857	5,788	74	100,413	1,884	53	328,444	3,887	85
Licenses	329,598	5,634	59	79,719	1,858	43	249,880	3,844	65
Federal duck stamps	16,578	850	20	2,675	137	20	13,902	713	20
Other stamps, tags, and permits	82,681	2,650	31	18,019	770	23	64,661	1,913	34

[1] Includes rifles, shotguns, ammunition, archery equipment, hunting dogs, etc.
[2] Includes camping equipment, binoculars, special clothing, taxidermy costs, etc.
[3] Includes boats, boat accessories, pickups, campers, cabins, 4-wheelers, etc.
* Based on a sample size of 21.
** Based on a sample size of 24.

Land Use

Land Use by Type of Game Hunters

In 2001 37% of all big game hunters used public land; 80% used private land. Small game hunters were similar, with 36% using public land and 80% using private land. Other animal (i.e., nongame such as coyotes, raccoons, and groundhogs) hunters had a lower percentage of public land use and a higher percentage of private land use, 27% and 86% respectively. Migratory bird hunters were the hunters who used private land the least with a 76% participation rate (although that is still over 3/4ths of all migratory bird hunters).

24% of big game hunting days were on public land; 72% were on private land (the remaining 4% were not reported by the Survey's respondents). Again, small game hunters mirrored big game hunters, with 27% of their days on public land and 70% on private land. 31% of migratory bird days were on public land and 67% on private land. Other animal hunters had a strong focus on private land hunting. 17% of their days were on public land and 84% on private land.

Owning and Leasing Hunting Land

In 2001 9%, or 981,000, of private land hunters owned hunting land, and 8%, or 904,000, leased hunting land. Private land hunters spent 86% of the total hunting landownership costs and 95% of the total hunting land leasing costs. On the other hand, 8%, or 403,000, of total public land hunters owned hunting land and 6%, or 317,000, of them leased hunting land. Public land hunters spent 56% of the total hunting landownership costs and 25% of the total hunting land leasing costs.

There was an obvious overlap between the public and private land hunting groups owning and leasing land. A total of 1,061,000 hunters owned land and 982,000 hunters leased land. 10%, or 328,000, of hunters who hunted on both public and private land owned hunting land and 8%, or 277,000, leased hunting land. 43% of land owning and 23% of land leasing costs were paid by hunters who used both private and public land. A significant proportion of people who leased and owned land for the primary purpose of hunting still hunted on public land.

As for people who hunted on private land only and others who hunted on public land only, the expectation is that private-land-only hunters would pay a large proportion of the total land leasing and owning costs and public-land-only hunters would pay a small proportion. Indeed, private-land-only hunters paid 43% of total hunting landownership costs and 72% of leasing land costs, while public-land-only hunters paid just 14% of landownership costs and 2% of leasing costs.

Regarding the trend in owning and leasing hunting land, in 1991 1.7 million hunters, 12% of all hunters, owned or leased hunting land. 853,000 owned hunting land (6% of all hunters) and 962,000 leased hunting land (7%). In 1996 1.6 million hunters, 12% of all hunters, owned or leased land, similar to 1991. And in 2001 1.7 million hunters, 13% of all hunters, owned or leased hunting land.

1.1 million hunters, 8% of all hunters, owned land and 982,000 hunters, 8% of all hunters, leased hunting land. Comparing 1991 to 2001, total expenditures and the total number of owning and leasing hunters have not changed despite the decline in hunting participation. Leasing expenditures are slightly higher in 2001 compared to 1991. Owning totals are slightly down.

In 1991 74% of land leasing and owning costs were paid by private-land-only hunters and 25% of costs were paid by hunters who used both public and private land. In 1996 64% were paid by private-land-only hunters and 31% were by public and private land hunters. In 2001 48% were paid by private-land-only hunters and 40% were paid by public and private land hunters. The trend in leasing and owning hunting land is more spending by those who hunt on both public and private land and less spending by private-land-only hunters.

Looking at leasing alone, in 1991 340,000 public land hunters spent money on leasing, averaging $361. In 2001 314,000 public land hunters spent money on leasing, averaging $505. As for private land hunters, in 1991 897,000 of them averaged $439 on leasing, and in 2001 885,000 averaged $670. Leasing prices were going up, but not the number of leasers. Leasing was becoming more important for the landowner who could charge the higher prices, but not more prevalent among hunters utilizing the leased land.

Regarding owning, in 1991 726,000 private land hunters averaged $4,802 and in 2001 869,000 averaged $3,317. So the reverse was true here: more hunters paid less per person for landownership for hunting. To complete the picture, 374,000 public land hunters averaged $2,373 for owning land in 1991, and 366,000 public land hunters averaged $5,167 in 2001. This was more like leasing, where the same number of participants was paying more over time.

Table 23. 2001 Land Owning/Leasing by Private Land Hunters
(Numbers in thousands.)

	Number	Percent
Total private land hunters	**10,724**	**100**
Who own hunting land	981	9
Who lease hunting land	904	8
Total hunting land ownership costs	**$3,351,389**	**100**
Amount spent for owning by private land hunters	$2,881,327	86
Total hunting land leasing costs	**$624,503**	**100**
Amount spent for leasing by private land hunters	$592,813	95

Table 24. 2001 Land Owning/Leasing by Public Land Hunters
(Numbers in thousands.)

	Number	Percent
Total public land hunters	**5,156**	**100**
Who own hunting land	403	8
Who lease hunting land	317	6
Total hunting land ownership costs	**$3,351,389**	**100**
Amount spent for owning by public land hunters	$1,890,522	56
Total hunting land leasing costs	**$624,503**	**100**
Amount spent for leasing by public land hunters	$158,555	25

Table 25. 2001 Land Owning/leasing by Hunters on Both Public and Private Land
(Numbers in thousands.)

	Number	Percent
Total public and private land hunters	**3,277**	**100**
Who own hunting land	328	10
Who lease hunting land	277	9
Total hunting land ownership costs	**$3,351,389**	**100**
Amount spent for owning by hunters using both public and private land	$1,431,366	43
Total hunting land leasing costs	**$624,503**	**100**
Amount spent for leasing by hunters using both public and private land	$144,535	23

Table 26. 2001 Land Owning/Leasing Expenditures by Private-Land-Only and Public-Land-Only Hunters
(Numbers in thousands.)

	Number	Percent
Owning expenditures		
Total hunting land ownership costs	**$3,351,389**	**100**
Public-land only hunters	$459,156	14
Private-land only hunters	$1,449,961	43
Leasing expenditures		
Total hunting land leasing costs	**$624,503**	**100**
Public-land only hunters	$14,020	2
Private-land only hunters	$448,278	72

Willingness to Pay

Deer, elk, and moose hunters were asked to estimate the most they would have been willing to pay for their hunting activity above that which they actually had to pay. This "consumer surplus" is the correct measure of the economic value of an activity. Looking at the willingness-to-pay estimates by public and private land hunters gives a good measure of the satisfaction people had with their various hunting experiences. See Figure 10 for a graphical depiction of the willingness-to-pay concept. "Net economic value" is another term for consumer surplus.

The highest gross willingness to pay (i.e., the actual expenditures plus the consumer surplus) average per big game hunting trip ($792) was by hunters who hunted on both public and private land. Interestingly, the next highest ($574) was public land hunters. Private land hunters would pay $457 per trip. Private-land-only hunters would pay $307, and public-land-only hunters would pay the lowest ($207).

The highest net economic value average for a big game hunting trip was by hunters who hunted on private land only, $274. Private land hunters were next, at $260. Hunters who hunted on both public and private land would pay $229 more than their actual expenditures. Public land hunters, $193, and public-land-only hunters, $132, brought up the rear.

The highest net willingness to pay per big game season (or per year) was $3,157, by hunters who hunted on both public and private land. The next highest ($2,839) was private land hunters. Private-land-only hunters had a consumer surplus of $2,696. Public land hunters would pay $2,135 per season more. Astoundingly, public-land-only hunters would pay only $428, by far the lowest. People who for whatever reason hunted only on public land did not value their hunting nearly as high as private land hunters. Another interpretation is those who value hunting the least didn't bother to obtain the privilege of hunting on private land.

Figure 10. Individual Hunter's Demand Curve for Hunting Trips

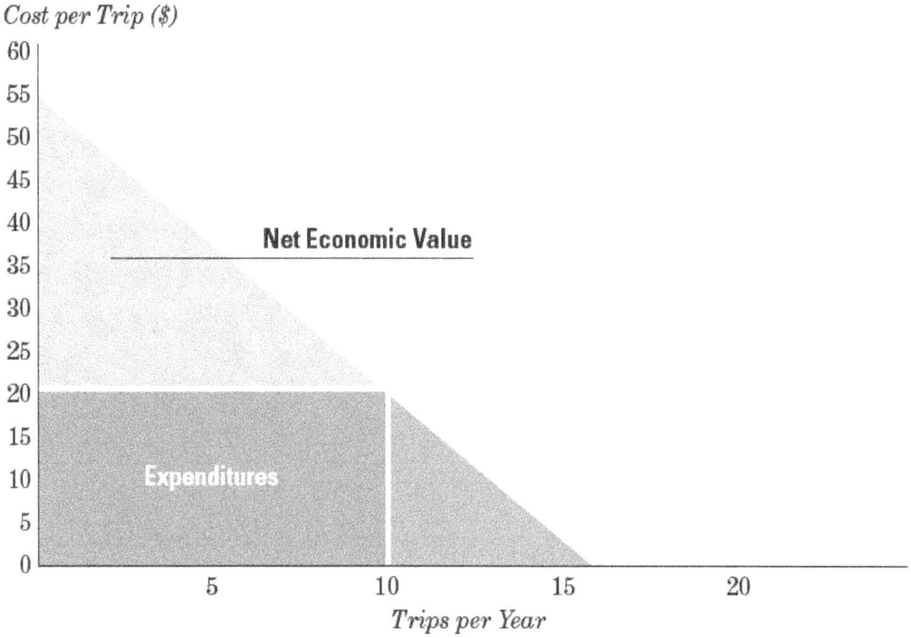

Table 27. Consumer Surplus Estimates for Big Game Hunting in 2001
(Participant averages. In 2001 dollars.)

	Gross Willingness to Pay per Trip	Net Willingness to Pay per Trip	Net Willingness to Pay Per Season
Private land hunters	$457	$260	$2,839
Private-land-only hunters	$307	$274	$2,696
Public and Private hunters	$792	$229	$3,157
Public land hunters	$574	$193	$2,135
Public-land-only hunters	$207	$132	$428
Public and Private hunters	$792	$229	$3,157

Summary

There is twice as much privately owned land as publicly owned land in the United States, and similarly there are twice as many hunters who use private land as hunters who use public land. A majority of hunters hunt on private land in all but a handful of states.

In 2001 private land hunters tended to specialize in private land use (69% of private land hunters hunted only on private land), whereas the majority of public land hunters hunted on private land as well (64% of public land hunters hunted on private land too). The trend over the years 1980 to 2001 was toward more private land hunting, particularly for big game hunters. Furthermore, on average private land hunters hunt more days than public land hunters.

From 1991 to 2001 the number of private land hunters declined along with overall hunter numbers, while public land hunters dropped at a rate twice as fast.

The hunting days trend tells a different story. The number of overall hunting days and its components public land days and private land days stayed relatively the same, with no statistically significant changes. There were fewer hunters, but those that remained took up the slack in effort afield.

The region of the country in which one lives is the most important determinant of whether public or private land are used for hunting. The only other significant socioeconomic characteristic differences between public and private land hunters were the rural/urban and female/male splits. Private land hunters tended to be more rural and included slightly more females.

Public land hunters spent more on average than private land hunters, but the participant who spent the most on average was the hunter who hunted on both private and public land, probably due to the relatively greater level of activity.

Big game hunters who used only private land valued their hunting higher than hunters who used only public land. This could be because the quality of hunting on private land was better, or because people who intrinsically value hunting more generally chose to hunt on private land, or both.

The trend of hunting in the U.S. is toward more private land use. Private landholders recognize that selling hunting rights on their land is a source of income, and some state fish and game agencies are pushing private land use for hunting. However, in 2001 about a third of all private land hunters used public land, in addition to the public-land-only hunters (14% of all hunters), so, particularly in the West, public land still plays an important role in hunting.

Table 28. Summary of Public and Private Land Use by Hunters in 2001
(Numbers in thousands.)

	All hunters	Percent	Private land only	Percent	Public land only	Percent	Private and public land	Percent
Hunters	13,034	100	7,447	57	1,879	14	3,277	25
Days hunted	228,368	100	115,841	51	21,899	10	86,978*	38
Expenditures	$20,611,025	100	$9,971,288	48	$2,438,194	12	$8,031,509	39

This is the number of days spent hunting by people who hunted on private and public land, not the number of days spent hunting on both private and public land.

Table 29. Average Expenditures by Public and Private Land Hunters in 2001
(Numbers in thousands, except averages.)

	Public land hunting	Private land hunting
Hunters	5,156	10,724
Expenditures	$10,469,703	$18,002,797
Average per hunter	$2,031	$1,679

Appendix I. The Most and Least Private Land Hunting, by State

States where private land hunters were 90% or more of all in-state hunters:

1991—AL, DE, GA, IL, IN, IA, KS, KY, ME, MS, MO, NE, NY, ND, OH, OK, SC, SD, TN, TX, VT, WV.

TOP NINE—NE 97%, IA 95%, TX 95%, KS 93%, KY 93%, MS 93%, MO 93%, ND 93%, OH 93%

1996—AL, DE, IN, IA, KS, KY, MS, MO, NE, NY, OH, OK, SC, TX.

TOP NINE—AL 95%, KS 95%, IA 93%, KY 93%, NY 93%, MS 92%, MO 92%, NE 92%, SC 92%

2001—AL, AR, KS, ME, MD, MS, MO, ND, OK, SC, SD, TN, TX, WV

TOP TEN—SD 108%, TN 95%, OK 94%, AL 93%, MS 92%, SC 92%, WV 92%, KS 91%, MO 91%, ND 91%

States where private land hunters were 50% or less of all in-state hunters:

1991—AK, AZ, CO, ID, NV, NM, OR, UT

BOTTOM THREE—AK 28%, AZ 30%, NM 32%

1996—AK, AZ, CO, ID, NV, NM, UT

BOTTOM THREE—AZ 22%, AK 25%, NV 33%

2001—AK, AZ, ID, NV, NM, OR, UT, WY

BOTTOM THREE—AK 19%, NM 27%, NV 28%

States where private land hunting days were 80% or more of all in-state hunting days:

1991—AL, GA, IL, IN, IA, KS, KY, ME, MS, NE, NH, NY, NC, OH, SD, TN, TX, VT, VA, WV.

TOP NINE—TX 94%, KY 91%, NE 91%, KS 90%, IA 89%, IL 87%, OH 87%, WV 87%, MS 85%

1996—FL, GA, IL, IN, IA, KS, KY, LA, ME, MS, MO, NE, NY, NC, OH, TX, VT, WV

TOP NINE—KS 108%, FL 100%, TX 100%, OH 99%, NC 96%, IA 94%, MS 94%, NE 93%, IL 91%

2001—AL, CT, DE, GA, IL, IN, KS, KY, ME, MD, MA, MS, MO, NE, NY, NC, ND, OH, OK, RI, SC, TN, TX, VT, VA, WV

TOP NINE—OK 111%, TX 106%, IN 98%, KY 98%, ME 98%, MO 98%, AL 97%, TN 97%, WV 97%

States where private land hunting days were 50% or less of all in-state hunting days:

1991—AK, AZ, CO, ID, MT, NV, NM, OR, UT, WA, WY

BOTTOM THREE—AZ 15%, AK 19%, NM 23%

1996—AK, AZ, CO, ID, NV, NM, OR, UT

BOTTOM THREE—AZ 15%, UT 17%, NV 19%

2001—AK, AZ, CO, ID, NV, NM, OR, UT, WA, WY

BOTTOM THREE—AK 17%, AZ 24%, NV 28%